FLORASPHERE

INSPIRED

Australian Wildflower
Colouring Book

CHERALYN DARCEY

ROCKPOOL
PUBLISHING

For my dearest friend Jan,
because if it wasn't for you,
my life would be a lot less colourful.

A Rockpool book
PO Box 252
Summer Hill
NSW 2130
Australia
www.rockpoolpublishing.com.au
http://www.facebook.com/RockpoolPublishing

ISBN 9781925017991

First published in 2015
Copyright © Cheralyn Darcey 2015
This edition published in 2015

Cover design by Jessica Le
Printed and bound in China

10 9 8 7 6 5 4 3 2 1

This Book Belongs to . . .

Below are the names and meanings of each of the Wildflowers featured in this colouring book as well as their individual energies.

Common Heath ~ *Epacris impressa* ~ *DIRECTION*

Cooktown Orchid ~ *Vappodes phalaenopsis* ~ *ATTITUDE*

Crowea ~ *Crowea exalata* ~ *POSSIBILITIES*

Geraldton Wax ~ *Chamelaucium uncinatum* ~ *ASSERTIVENESS*

Golden Wattle ~ *Acacia pycnantha* ~ *JOY*

Grevillea ~ *Grevillea banksii* ~ *CREATIVITY*

Gymea Lily ~ *Doryanthes excela* ~ *AWARENESS*

Lechenaultia ~ *Lechenaultia formasa* ~ *SUCCESS*

Native Passion Flower ~ *Passiflora herbertiana* ~ *LOVE*

Rabbit Orchid ~ *Leptoceras menziesii* ~ *ABUNDANCE*

Swamp Lily ~ *Crinum pedunculatum* ~ *ENERGY*

Tea Tree ~ *Leptospermum myrsinoides* ~ *ATTAINMENT*

Turkey Bush ~ *Calytrix exstipulata* ~ *INSPIRATION*

Violet Nightshade ~ *Solanum brownii* ~ *POWER*

Waratah ~ Telopea speciosissima ~ SURVIVAL

INTRODUCTION

Let go and colour to your heart's content. Let the flowers quietly fill your life with their gifts.

This is a colouring book containing Australian flowers created especially for you to help you connect with calmness, healing and gentle guidance.

I adore art, botany, gardening – anything to do with plants. They capture my imagination and fascination to learn more. When I write my books and card decks, along with magazine articles, I keep rather extensive journals and sketchbooks. It is while keeping these that I am always aware of the patterns and the textures of nature and how they make me feel.

In our day-to-day lives we tend to overlook the beauty that is already here in order to find something we think is more special, more different and new. All we need do is stop and look again. It is through doing this myself that I have visualised what I call 'Floraspheres': small patterned shapes, usually circular, made of the geometry and repeated patterns of what I find while sketching and observing nature.

You will recognise leaves, petals, seeds, berries, roots and more details of Australian flowers in each of the following Floraspheres. I encourage you to colour them in any way your heart desires. Play, relax, explore and find yourself in nature's rhythms. You may also wish to select a flower that focuses on the way you feel or would like to feel on any given day.

Use any medium you wish. There are no rules that come with colouring each Florasphere, just an invitation to be you.

The flowers' meanings (to the left) are based on traditional flower and plant reading, which links with aromatherapy and with flower essences, and they may bring a little of their energy into your day as well.

I have also created a dedicated website filled with resources and community for you at **www.florasphere.com**

May Nature always bless you and may you also be a blessing to Nature.

CAN YOU FIND THE WILDFLOWERS?

Can you find the Australian Wildflowers?
Each of the colouring pages is created from a single Wildflower. These are the
drawings from my sketchbooks that became the inspiration for each Florasphere.
Can you find which Wildflower is contained in the Floras

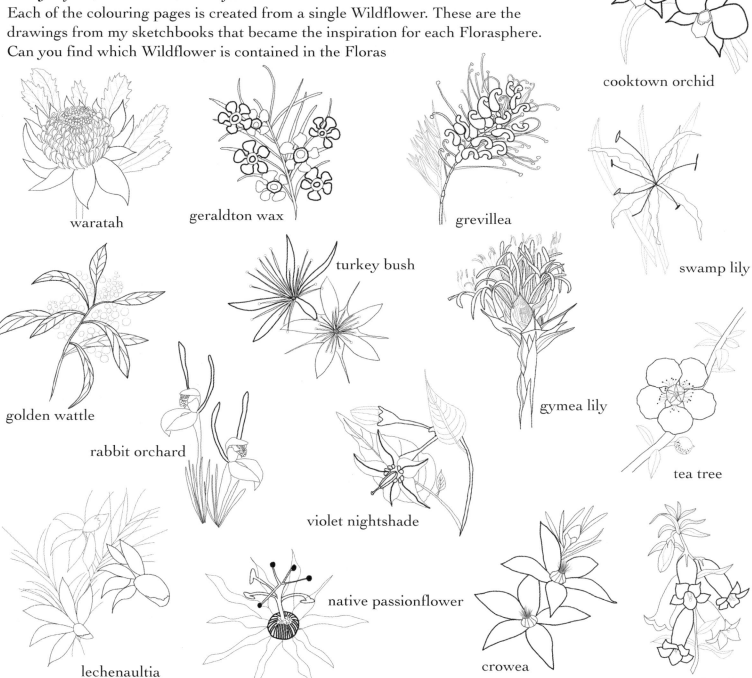

cooktown orchid

waratah

geraldton wax

grevillea

swamp lily

turkey bush

golden wattle

gymea lily

rabbit orchard

tea tree

violet nightshade

lechenaultia

native passionflower

crowea

common heath

'Normality is a paved road: it's comfortable to walk, but no flowers
grow on it.'
Vincent Van Gogh

'When you take a flower in your hand and really look at it, it's your world for the moment. I want to give that world to someone else. Most people in the city rush around so, they have no time to look at a flower. I want them to see it whether they want to or not.'

Georgia O'Keeffe

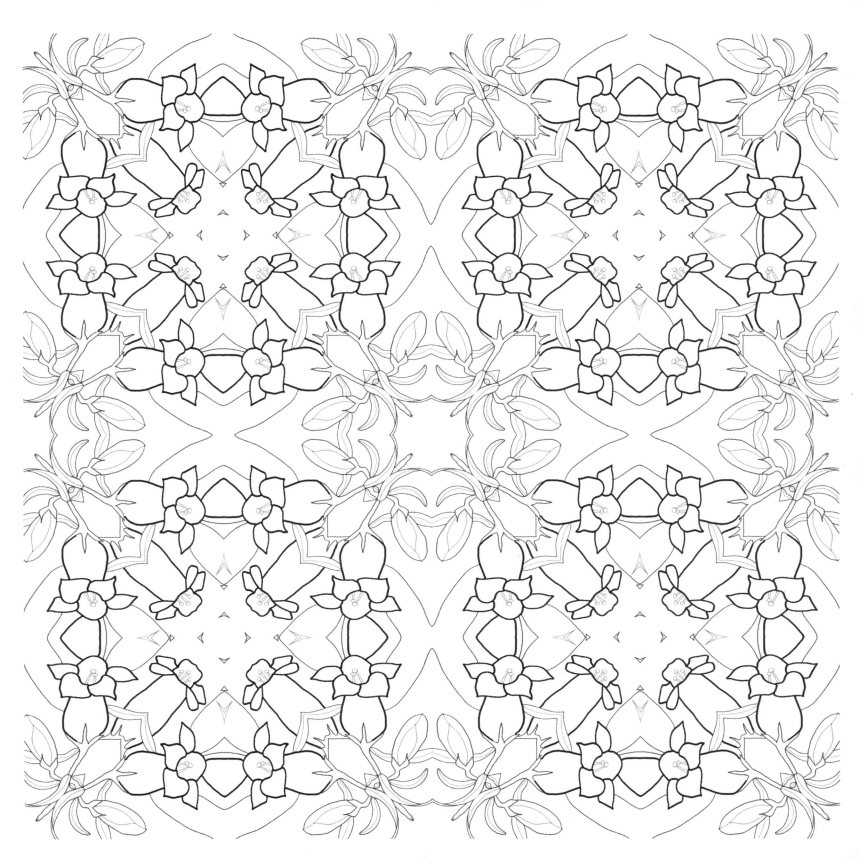

'Be like the flower, turn your face to the sun.'
Kahlil Gibran

'I'd rather have roses on my table than diamonds on my neck.'
__Emma Goldman__

'The earth laughs in flowers.'
Ralph Waldo Emerson

'To the artist there is never anything ugly in nature.'
Auguste Rodin

'A flower does not think of competing with the flower next to it.
It just blooms.'
Zen Shin

'Don't judge each day by the harvest you reap but by the seeds that you plant.'
Robert Louis Stevenson

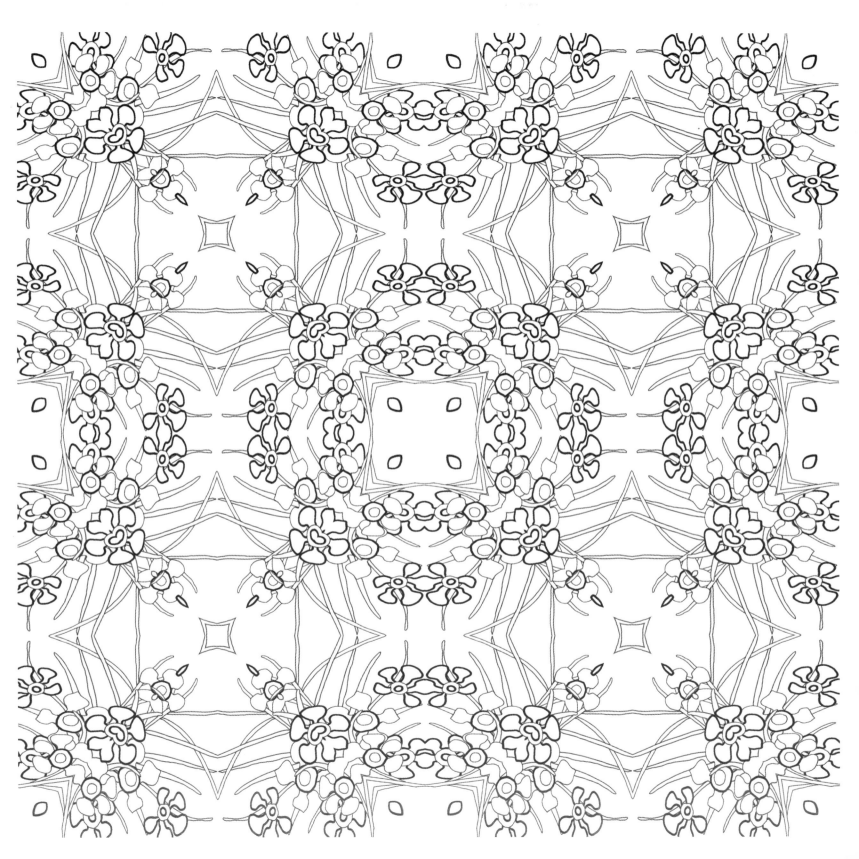

'Whoever loves and understands a garden will find contentment within.'
Chinese Proverb

'When one tugs at a single thing in nature, he finds it attached
to the rest of the world.'

John Muir

'There came a time when the risk to remain tight in the bud was more painful than the risk it took to blossom.'

Anäis Nin

'I have never had so many good ideas day after day as when
I worked in the garden.'
John Erskine

'What's in a name? That which we call a rose. By any other name would smell as sweet.'

Shakespeare, *Romeo and Juliet*

'The actual flower is the plant's highest fulfilment, and are not here exclusively for herbaria, county floras and plant geography: they are here first of all for delight.'

John Ruskin

'I perhaps owe having become a painter to flowers.'
Claude Monet

'In all things of nature there is something of the marvellous.'
Aristotle

'More grows in the garden than the gardener sows.'
Spanish Proverb

'Nature is a writer's best friend.'
Agavé Powers

'Plant a seed of friendship. Reap a bouquet of happiness.'
Lois L. Kaufman

'The flower is the poetry of reproduction. It is an example of the eternal seductiveness of life.'

Jean Giraudoux

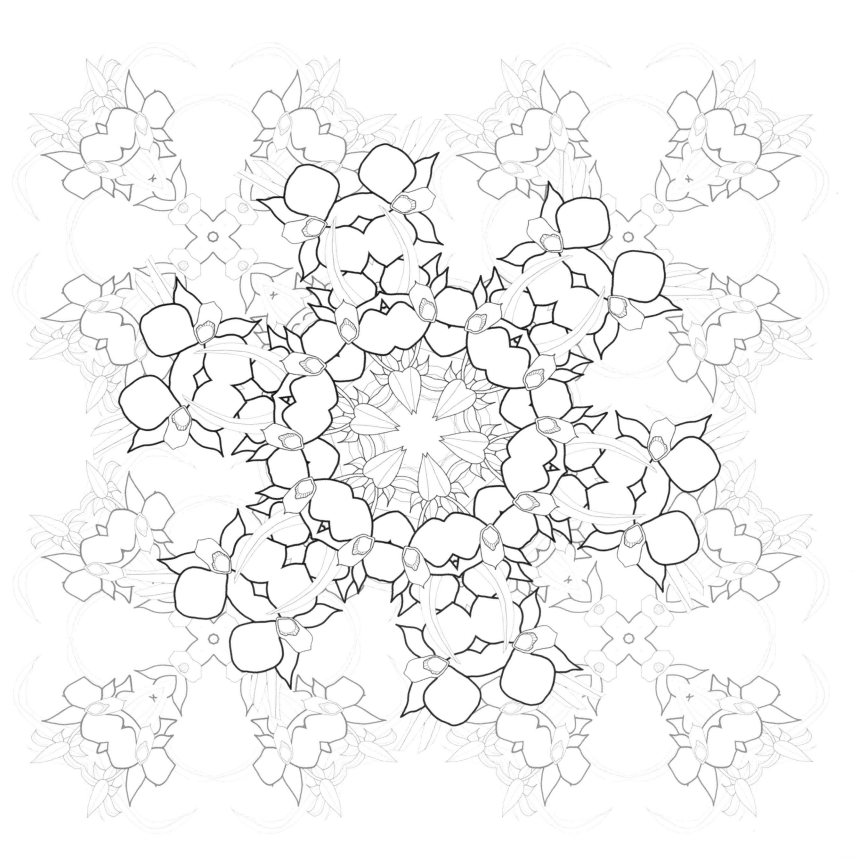

'You're the perfect gardener for this flower.'
Unknown

'None can have a healthy love for flowers unless he loves the wild ones.'

Forbes Watson

'It will never rain roses: when we want to have more roses, we must plant more roses.'

George Eliot

'All the flowers of all the tomorrows are in the seeds of today'
Indian Proverb

'The first blooms of spring always make my heart sing.'
S. Brown

'Every child is born a naturalist. His eyes are, by nature, open to the glories of the stars, the beauty of the flowers, and the mystery of life.'

Ritu Ghatourey

'There is material enough in a single flower for the ornament of
a score of cathedrals.'
__John Ruskin__

'In the spring, at the end of the day, you should smell like dirt.'
Margaret Atwood

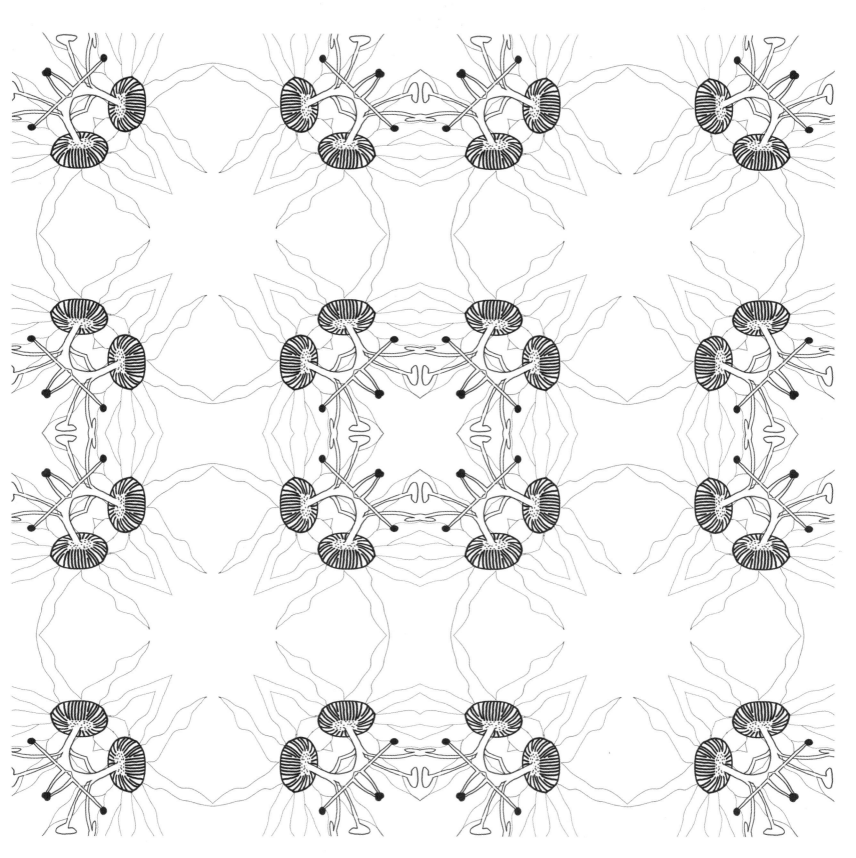

'Every flower must grow through dirt.'
Laurie Jean Sennott

'Nothing is more completely the child of art than a garden.'
Sir Walter Scott

'People from a planet without flowers would think we must be mad with joy the whole time to have such things about us.'
Dame Iris Murdoch

'Won't you come into the garden? I would like my roses to see you.'
Richard Sheridan

'One touch of nature makes the whole world kin.'
William Shakespeare

'There is not a sprig of grass that shoots uninteresting to me.'
Thomas Jefferson

'Bloom where you're planted!'
Mary Engelbreit

'Art is the unceasing effort to compete with the beauty of
flowers – and never succeeding.'
Gian Carlo Menotti

'Some people worry that artificial intelligence will make us feel inferior, but then, anybody in his right mind should have an inferiority complex every time he looks at a flower.'

Alan C. Kay

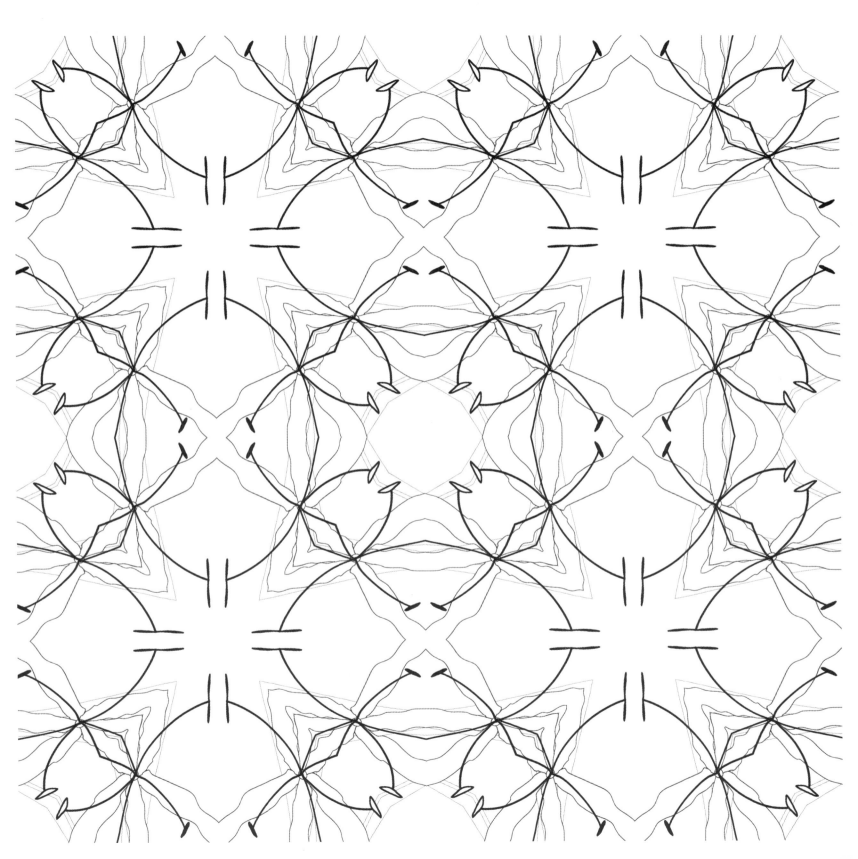

'A flower blossoms for its own joy.'
Oscar Wilde

'I stress the uniqueness of the Australian landscape and its metaphysical and mythic content.'

Arthur Boyd

'A flower's appeal is in its contradictions – so delicate in form yet strong in fragrance, so small in size yet big in beauty, so short in life yet long on effect.'
Terri Guillemets

'Joy is a flower that blooms when you do.'
Anonymous

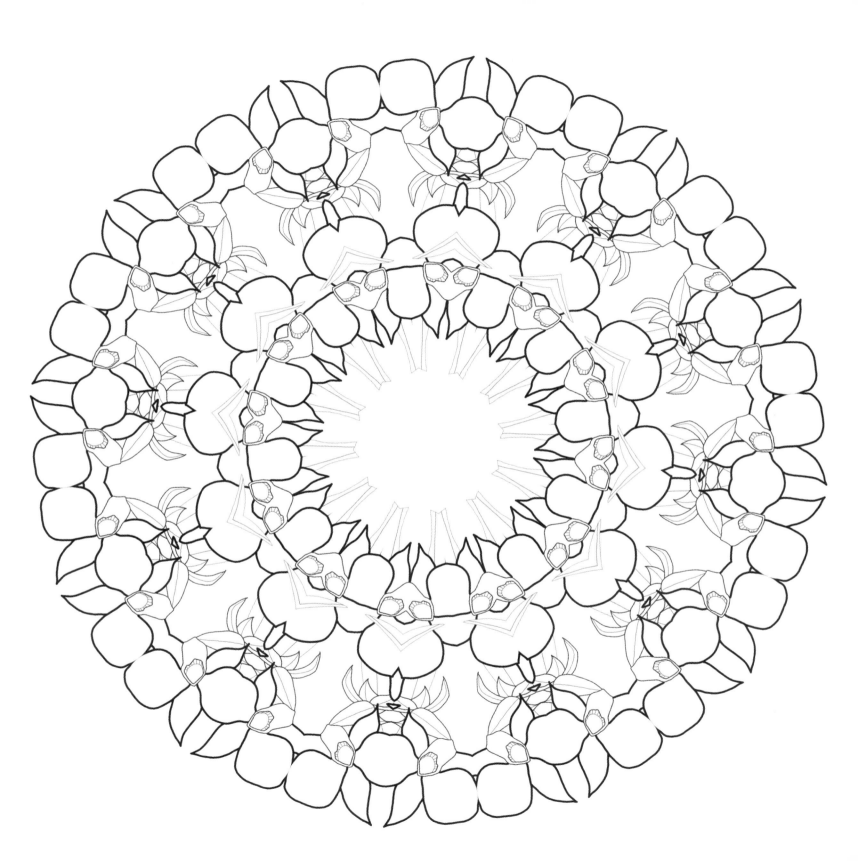

'I love a sunburnt country, a land of sweeping plains
Of ragged mountain ranges, of droughts and flooding rains.'
Dorothea Mackellar

'Flowers never emit so sweet and strong a fragrance as before a storm.
When a storm approaches thee, be as fragrant as a sweet-smelling flower.'
Jean Paul Richter

'He is happiest who hath power to gather wisdom from a flower.'
Mary Howitt

'Spring has returned. The Earth is like a child that knows poems.'
Rainer Maria Rilke

'Nobody sees a flower really; it is so small it takes time. We haven't time, and to see takes time – like to have a friend takes time.'
Georgia O'Keeffe

'A fairy seed I planted, so dry and white and old, there sprang a vine enchanted, with magic flowers of gold.'
Marjorie Barrows

'I hope that while so many people are out smelling the flowers, someone is taking the time to plant some.'
Herbert Rappaport

'To create a little flower is the labor of ages.'
William Blake

'It's the colours, the light, the space. It's really very deep in my soul …
In the Australian bush and inland deserts, there is a sense of being
the first person in a place.'

Suzanne Cory

'Happiness held is the seed. Happiness shared is the flower.'
John Harrigan

'And the sun sank again on the grand Australian bush – the nurse and tutor of eccentric minds, the home of the weird, and of much that is different from things in other lands.'

Henry Lawson

'Do you suppose she's a wildflower?'
Lewis Carroll, *Alice's Adventures in Wonderland*

'Life begins the day you start a garden.'
Chinese Proverb

'No seed shall perish which the soul hath sown.'
John Addington Symonds

'Deep in their roots, all flowers keep the light.'
Theodore Roethke

'To forget how to dig the earth and to tend the soil is to forget ourselves.'
Mahatma Gandhi

'You will find something more in woods than in books. Trees and stones will teach you that which you can never learn from masters.'
St. Bernard de Clairvaux

'Let us dance in the sun, wearing wild flowers in our hair...'
Susan Polis Shutz

Florasphere Calm
Cheralyn Darcey

A special collection of favourite calming Australian Wildflowers.
All uniquely hand drawn, you will delight in finding sweet
Flannel Flowers to the gentle Kangaroo Paws in every intricate,
peace-induced geometric kaleidoscope. Let the beauty and the
calming energy of nature overtake you as you colour in each
beautifully illustrated page, which can be treasured whole or
removed to frame your favourite flower.
ISBN: 9781925017977
RRP $16.99

Available at all good bookstores or online at
www.rockpoolpublishing.com.au

Australian Wildflower Reading Cards

Cheralyn Darcey

In every card, on every page, in every word, in every picture the Australian wildflowers will speak to you – soul to soul. Featuring 44 cards and a guidebook with unique flower spreads for readings and a special card of the day as well as instructions. These cards will delight those that love beautiful oracle tools and traditional artwork.

ISBN: 9781925017243

RRP $24.99

Flower Reading Cards

Cheralyn Darcey

If you have ever wondered what a flower means or why anyone has ever attributed symbolic meaning to a plant then this card set will answer those questions.
The ancient art of reading flowers and plants for divination and for healing insight, is gained through understanding these meanings so that you may wish them on others or bring that energy into your own world.

ISBN: 9781925017588

RRP $24.99

Available at all good bookstores or online at
www.rockpoolpublishing.com.au

Cheralyn Darcey is an environmental artist and Flower
Reader who has a lifelong connection with the study of
the relationship between people and plants. Though her
work she has slowly rekindled the ancient tradition
of Flower Reading, (Floramancy). Cheralyn's art has
featured in workshops, exhibitions, art prizes and
publications internationally.

Cheralyn Darcey is the author and illustrator of
the *Australian Wildflower Reading Cards* and the
Flower Reading Cards.

www.florasphere.com
www.twitter.com/florasphere
www.facebook.com/florasphere
www.instagram.com/florasphere